Turn Up the Ocean

Turn Up the Ocean

~ poems ~

Tony Hoagland

Graywolf Press

This publication is made possible, in part, by the voters of Minnesota through a Minnesota State Arts Board Operating Support grant, thanks to a legislative appropriation from the arts and cultural heritage fund. Significant support has also been provided by the McKnight Foundation, the Lannan Foundation, the Amazon Literary Partnership, and other generous contributions from foundations, corporations, and individuals. To these organizations and individuals we offer our heartfelt thanks.

Published by Graywolf Press
212 Third Avenue North, Suite 485
Minneapolis, Minnesota 55401

www.graywolfpress.org

Published in the United States of America

ISBN 978-1-64445-092-5 (paperback)
ISBN 978-1-64445-180-9 (ebook)

2 4 6 8 9 7 5 3 1
First Graywolf Printing, 2022

Library of Congress Control Number: 2021945918

Cover design: Kyle G. Hunter

Cover art: Konen Uehara, *Hatō Zu*. Library of Congress, Prints & Photographs Division [LC-DIG-jpd-01826].

CONTENTS

Turn Up the Ocean

BIBLE ALL OUT OF ORDER

One thing's for sure; in the future, the morgues are going to be full of tattoos.
It's going to be more colorful and easier to manage:
"Hey Jeff, move Dolphin-Shoulder-Girl to tray seven."
"And get Mr. Flames-on-My-Neck out for the doc."

In Italy the tabloids are talking about *L'Ambulanza della Morte*,
the Ambulance of Death;
a medic who was killing his passengers
to provide business for his brother's funeral parlor.

I think we can agree that the world is a Bible
with the chapters shuffled all out of order.
I think we still can't decide which we want
in the end: Justice or Mercy.

When my doctor asks what my symptoms are, I tell her
self-pity and a desire to apologize.
She says my insurance policy covers self-pity,
but not, unfortunately, remorse.

Remember the movie in which Sidney Poitier plays a school teacher
who returns the love letter from one of his students,
returns it with all the grammatical errors
corrected in red, heartbreaking ink?

I'm sometimes afraid that's what I've done with life.

Yet here's what I have to say to all you travelers—
Moses doesn't make it to the Promised Land.
Cain and Abel don't get reunited in the end.
Belief is not a requirement to go on living.
It's possible I have this all out of order.

We'll end up at a funeral parlor run by somebody's brother,
our bodies covered with scars and invisible ink.
While I'm lying there naked, flat on my back,
I hope I remember all that I went through—
the storms and the lovers and mountains;

complaining at the top of my lungs;
salting my grief with my mirth
while being tossed this way and that, askew and asunder,
in this blithering whirlwind of wonder.

GORGON

Now that you need your prescription glasses to see the stars
and now that the telemarketers know your preference in sexual positions.

Now that corporations run the government
and move over the land like giant cloud formations.

Now that the human family has turned out to be a conspiracy against
    the planet.

Now that it's hard to cast stones
without hitting a cell-phone tower,
which will show up later on your bill.

Now that you know you are neither innocent nor powerful
nor a character in a book.

You have arrived at the edge of the world
where the information wind howls incessantly

and you stand in your armor made of irony
with your sword of good intentions raised—

The world is a Gorgon.
It presents its thousand ugly heads.

Death or madness to look at it too long,
but your job
is not to conquer it;

not to provide entertaining repartee,
nor to revile yourself in shame.

Your job is to stay calm.
Your job is to watch and take notes,
to go on looking.

Your job is to not be turned into stone.

IMMERSION

That was a beautiful silence in the house,
when my mother was dying in the spring:
just the sound of breathing in the dark bedroom,

heavy and slow, like the pump of a compressor,
as if she was a diver who had gone far down
and wished to stay there in the dark for good.

Ah, that was a great adventure.
Then didn't we feel her under us,
in her fins and mask, deep in the abyss,

feeling her way from submerged room to room
among the carved inscriptions of sarcophagi,
past the great stone faces of the flooded pyramids?

While up on the surface
we performed the tasks we had been given;
watching the instruments and dials,

adjusting the tethers and lines,
tracking her movement through
passageways and crypts;

as she, on her business,
like some terrible Houdini,
worked her disentanglement

and we floated on the waves in unison,
immersed in the tide of her breath,
and listened to her moving down there, in and out

and then a little forward
like a great whale
slowly headed outbound

with a kind of royalty.

DISCLOSURE AGREEMENT

Before I came to work on this planet
I signed a nondisclosure agreement with god
that I would not publicly discuss
what goes on around this place

—the cockroaches in the waiting room, for example;
that most angels have bad breath;
the low statistical success rate
of the surgery for transplanting souls.

I admit that I filled out those documents myself,
but why would I honor a contract with an employer like that,
who wastes so many and saves so few,
who ignores the terrible things that they let themselves do?

I have plenty to tell the tabloids if they ever show up:
about the nasty infection called "achieving success,"
what they are willing to put up for sale,
the precious things that they throw away.

What drives me most nuts of all, I suppose,
is the way they believe they are real.

Still I wish to acknowledge the sunlight and wind
and the strength of the trees, which live up to their rep.
When I look out the window
and see a golden field in the afternoon light
swaying in the breeze like a lion's mane—

I can see it's possible I have made a mistake.
I can see that it's possible I have constructed
this story of disappointment and grief:
the song of abandonment I was trained to expect.

I just want you to know I haven't given up.
I'm still searching for the message that
I've heard so much about;
I'd like to look at a boat or a bird without thinking of escape.

I should and I must be more patient.
I must believe that sticking around
is the only way I have to become a human being.

I promise—I'm going to work hard;
but I'm not telling anyone what I see in the future,
nor where I plan to go after this,
and I won't give anyone my true name even when asked,
and I'm not going to sign anything ever again.

BOTANY

When we met, I pretended to know a lot about botany,
and I called the trees *palmettos* and the flowers *spiderwort*
though I have no idea what spiderwort looks like
or even if such a thing really exists.

When I told you that a new species
has just been named after the Bee Gees,
I could sense that you were kind of interested,

so I kept making up other celebrity orchids,
like the Joan Baez and the Pink Floyd,
the Mahalia Jackson and the Al Green.

I have always loved the way that words
themselves have shape and color,
crimson tassels and dark-green fans
to catch the sun and rain,

and when I pick the words out as I speak,
sometimes I feel like I am making
a bouquet for you, arranging them in
a little turquoise vase for presentation.

That is why, in the name of honesty, I want to tell you
it is not true that Montreal roses
were my mother's favorite flower.
I don't know why I said that, it just flew out of my mouth,

but I hope you will still come over
to my apartment on the weekend,
so I can show you the spatula plants in my backyard
and maybe the leopard ferns in their shimmery autumn blossom.

If not, I am afraid that I will spend my life
alone, with nothing but these words,
touching them restlessly over and over,
bored and despairing

since it seems that I have loved them—
I mean the words—
better and more honestly
than I have ever loved a person.

WHY I LIKE THE HOSPITAL

Because it is all right to be in a bad mood there,
slouching along through the underground garage,
riding wordlessly on the elevator with the other customers,
staring at the closed beige doors like a prison wall.

I like the hospital for the way it grants permission for pathos
—the mother with cancer deciding how to tell her kids,
the bald girl gazing downward at the shunt
installed above her missing breast,

the crone in her pajamas, walking with an IV pole.
I don't like the smell of antiseptic,
or the air-conditioning set on high all night,
or the fresh flowers tossed into the wastebaskets,

but I like the way some people on their plastic chairs
break out a notebook and invent a complex scoring system
to tally up their days on earth,
the column on the left that says, *Times I Acted Like a Fool*,
facing the column on the right that says, *Times I Acted Like a Saint.*

I like the long prairie of the waiting;
the forced intimacy of the self with the self;
each sick person standing in the middle of a field,
like a tree wondering what happened to the forest.

And once I saw a man in a lime-green dressing gown,
hunched over in a chair; a man who was not
yelling at the doctors, or pretending to be strong,
or making a murmured phone call to his wife,

but one sobbing without shame,
pumping it all out from the bottom of the self,

the overflowing bilge of helplessness and rage,
a man no longer expecting to be saved,

but if you looked, you could see
that he was holding his own hand in sympathy,
listening to every single word,
and he was telling himself everything.

SQUAD CAR LIGHT

Too bad you have to be arrested to really find out what it is
or to be standing next to someone who is getting arrested
when the cops arrive in their ponderous vehicles—

the cruiser parked on your neighbor's weedy lawn,
the beacon bathing the whole neighborhood
the cold color of a cherry popsicle,

and the officers—so much gear attached to them,
they clank when they walk—the spurs and handcuffs
hung from their belts,
the slender baton for administering shock.

This was the light that splashed the leaves
that night in the Garden of Gethsemane,
the night they came to fetch the teacher,

and spread him on the hood of his own car
—while the neighbors watched from
behind their flowered curtains

and the disciples slipped into the dark.
And now you must be starting to understand
what a vain idea it was

to call yourself a brother of mankind
because now all you want is to be safe;
all you want is to be well out of sight.

For the rest of your life you'll remember
this terrible red light, splashing the trees and the houses.
Remember the night when your fear woke up.

Remember the ones you let go in your place.
Remember the ones all over the world
who are raising their arms right now,

then putting their wrists behind their backs;
finding out what it means to be chosen
and frozen

by squad car light.

TURN UP THE OCEAN

Now that I've bought a machine that plays noises recorded from nature,
I can have *Thunderstorm* or *Forest Pines* or *Sonorous Ocean*
at the push of a button.

It soothes me in the night to hear the waves
sweeping over the beach again and again
and the blue-gray background screech of the gulls.

It turns out this sound is all the comfort I ever wanted
and that all the conversation I really need
is that surging of surf played on a permanent loop.

Who knew the ocean could be kept on a digital chip
along with *Morning Birdsong*
and *Wind through Summer Grass?*

Again and again my heart has been broken
by people who didn't have what I want;
whom I then accused of refusing

to give me all that they had.
When their only fault, I now see,
was not being the trees or the wind or the rain,

which are only generous because
they have an endless supply of everything.
Their crime was not being everything, those people,

which it turns out was my crime too.
Now when I hear myself complaining,
I can say, "This pattern of mine has a certain repetition,"

which, who knows, someday might even seem natural.
In the meantime, I'm going to rely
on the great outdoors,

which I keep in my little room,
where I'm going to turn up the ocean.

THE REASON HE BROUGHT HIS GUN TO SCHOOL: A BLUES

Well, what the fuck did you expect?
His daddy was a Texaco,
his momma was a commercial for athletic shoes.

The breast milk he drank was Coca-Cola
and his balls
were some of those Styrofoam peanuts
that come as packing material in boxes for catalog shopping.

He was born between the fried chicken franchise and the 7-Eleven,
on the night of the made-for-TV movie
in which a hit man for the Mafia
falls in love with a lady cop.

The only obstetrician in attendance
was a semitruck full of exercise equipment
passing on Route 66

and the zodiac above his delivery
was a malt-liquor billboard
programmed to play mariachi music.

His character was a fraction
        formed by mornings of evangelist radio
divided by a flock of high school girls
        in tank tops and too-tight shorts.

If he had read the *Odyssey*,
        he might have tried to stop his ears;
if he had read the small print on the prescription-pill bottle,
        he might have gagged or blindfolded himself,

but how could he know?
He was a classic piece of American lunch meat
caught between two slices of white noise
        in a club sandwich of confusion.

What could you expect
but the skulking pent-up resentment of a chained dog
        tormented out of its wits.

And how could you really be surprised
when he found his imagination in a gun
        and picked it up
and pretended it was real.

BUTTER

I think it was Marie who first taught me the art
of spreading flattery on people
then smearing it around like marmalade on slabs of whole wheat bread,

or how to spray them lightly with a mist of unexpected praise
from one of those special nozzles
you attach to the end of your garden hose.

Walking around with her that year, I watched how she would

lubricate the world
—nuns and firemen, nannies and human resource managers,
nine-year-old kids in city playgrounds,
and widows selling flags in Central Park.

Pretty soon I started doing it myself,
telling this person and that how good they looked today;

how rare it is to see a job well done;
how excellent their taste in clothes.

I liked the way even the most crusty and resistant
at first would startle under the assault
then start to flourish under the effect.

I liked to watch the moisture trickle down to their roots
and then roll back up again
to all four corners of the leaf.

Why did I ever think that approval was gratuitous?
Why did it take me so long to see that the power of sweetness
is as great as the power of the river and the sun?

If I can't improve the world by scorching it with truth,
if I can't conquer it by twisting its arm behind its back,

then give me some adjectives like lipstick and gloss,
give me some language like mint and honey for the heart.

I will lavish the world with the power of butter.
I will force it to feel good about itself.

First I will make it blush—
then I will step back, and watch it shine.

DIAGNOSIS

It's not that I need to tell *everyone* I meet that I have cancer,
but standing in the checkout lane at Albertson's, I do feel a definite urge
to casually tell maybe just the cashier and the sixty-five-year-old bag boy,

and at the dentist's office it slips out almost accidentally
while I am discussing the latest breakthroughs in flossing
with the receptionist.
I tell her, "They aren't making any promises."

It would be too melodramatic and Keatsian
to stop by the graveyard on my way home
and stroll in broad daylight among the stones and names—

but I might go by my neighbor's
and visit the pet goat in the backyard,
tethered there in summer to keep the landscape manageable.

"Just keep it to yourself," I tell her, "I don't want this getting out,"
knowing that she will gaze at me with her giant green-gray glossy eyes
as she continues her unceasing mastication.

It is true that I sent many people in my life away
because I couldn't bear for them to be so close—
is it possible that now that trend has been reversed?

Or would it be more accurate to say I want to scrape my bad news
off on them in order to get rid of it
like something yucky stuck on the bottom of a shoe

and have the veneer of my disbelief restored?

It reminds me of the scene in the Greek epic underworld,
where the dead fighter Anteus is standing
on the wooden bridge between the living and the dead—

looking around and trying to decide what to do

until the concierge asks him politely,
could he please at least step aside
because there are others waiting to cross this bridge.

And he says, "Why don't they just go?"
And he says, "Because you are standing in their way."

And he says, "But I don't see them."
And he says, "Yes, your diagnosis is the same
as it has always been:

They are here and you don't see them.
But they see you."

NATURE IS STRONG

Put a bald truck tire in the top of a cypress tree in Florida
and soon an osprey will arrive to build its roost
of sharp dry twigs and torn-up winter grass.

Nature is strong.
It feels good to say that: "Nature is strong."
After the nine species of moth

that carried the fine yellow pollen from one vine to the next
at the edge of the forest in Belize—
after all nine species have been declared extinct,

a tenth species will appear.
The last known example of the slippery frog
with its slick lemon skin and its lily-pad toes

will be discovered under the hood
of a rusty Rolls-Royce in a garage
because nature is strong.

The humans will whisper that the end is near,
the young mother pushing the stroller through the mall
will feel an inexplicable despair.

The linguist will read a book called *How to Be Happy*,
turn the last page and be no happier.
The cities may be underwater,
the drowned still adrift in their cars,

but the monkey will go down to the river,
find a rock shaped like a spatula,
and start to dig in the sand,

and the lavender jellyfish will pulse and unpulse
its glowing abdominal sac
through the dark of the Atlantic
like a letter en route in the mail

—strange, strange, strange,
                      and strong.

ILLNESS AND LITERATURE

In those cold rooms with the blue plastic chairs,
sometimes the human condition
is an old Texas redneck with a brushy mustache
reading a Louis L'Amour novel
while waiting for his chemotherapy;
this tough old man who ran an auto-parts store for years,
then bought a whole chain of auto-parts stores,
who sits now furiously reading
about fistfights and saloons,
as the cattle drive heads into Wyoming,
to the summer pastures in the big sky country.

The schoolmarm buys two yards of calico in the general store
and the drunken sheriff gathers up his nerve
for the public gunfight in the dusty street,
while the cancer keeps plowing, plowing, plowing,
on a small piece of land just west of town;
while the owner of the valley, and of the whole darn territory,

is this leathery old Texan, in the blue plastic chair
who shifts from his left buttock to his right,
tugs at his mustache and turns the page.
He has a long way to go—he's got to get to Abilene
before they hang the wrong man.
Now, hearing his name called from the clinic door,
he stands, and walks into the hot, dry wind,
his spurs ringing on the polished floor.

"ON A SCALE OF 1–10," SAID THE NURSE, "HOW WOULD YOU RATE YOUR PAIN TODAY?"

If 1 is the name of your best friend from sixth grade,
which, for no reason, you remember right now,
standing in your socks on the cold tile of the examination room

—and 2 is how you will find your car in the parking lot later
and notice how dirty it has become—the back seat littered
with plastic wrappers and sales receipts—
and how it seems like a statement of how you have lived your life.

If 4 is the ache you feel in your left jaw
from clenching your teeth for the last ten years,
much in the manner of your father,

and 5 is what you felt at midnight last week
when you saw the flashing red lights of a police car
rolled up on your next-door neighbor's lawn,

splashing the whole street the sickening
color of strawberry jello
as their son was handcuffed, locked in the back, and driven away.

If 6 is the quiet discomfort you feel about being
a citizen of the richest country on earth
—which seems to be dragging you along for the ride,
a ride to which you do not seem to be objecting
as you enter the all-natural grocery store.

If 8 is the absence of a parent or brother or child
whom you might call at this moment
to explain where you are.

If 9 is your loss of belief in sense-making itself
combined with the slight nausea you get
when you try to arrange things in ascending order,

then how do you measure that?
What is its numerical value?

BANDAGE

Down in the pocket of this old green pair of pants
I find a dirty, wadded-up bandage
with a rusty coin-size stain in the cotton pad,

hidden where I shoved it during one of those days
when I was going to the clinic every few weeks
getting a bag of steroids and gemcitabine

pumped through the tip of a needle—
like a bombing mission aimed at a town
in a foreign country—

call it Kidneystan or West Pancreas—
I haven't worn these pants since, I guess,
having lost enough weight that they no longer fit

and it's strange to find this little memoir
of the harrowing winter
so pure in its intensity

—driving downtown in the rainy dawn,
everything crumbling, nothing fixed or solid anymore—
half breaking down

while singing along to the radio.
It wasn't hard to see the weeping itself
as a kind of mercy,

as it is mercy now to hold up this scrap
between my forefinger and thumb,
and to look at the spot of rusty old blood

on the rubberized cloth
like a little sunset, reddish and smudged,
I can stare into now

only if I raise my hand
to shield my eyes
from the dark.

AMERICAN STORY

Then it is spring break for the American colleges:
the roads to the coast are flooded with cars

and the quiet beaches are suddenly filled with drunken college boys
from Wisconsin and Connecticut
trying to pick up drunken coeds from Virginia and Chattanooga.

By six the sunburn ointment is gone from the shelves,
by eight the sidewalk bars are jammed,
the beer spigots are pumping like oil wells,

and by nine o'clock the guys have already started leaping
from the second-floor motel balconies
into the kidney-shaped swimming pool below,

splashing the chemical-blue water over the patio furniture,
as the girls in their halter tops
stand shrieking and begging the boys to stop.

But all the screams do is drive the wet boys
up the stairs again faster,
to jump from the next level up, and then to start with the tricks—
doing the Tarzan yell, trying the backward flip.

Nobody knows if the inevitable will happen,
but everybody understands when it does:
how the foot of the boy finally slips

on the greasy balcony rail;
then the cartwheeling fall, the body twisting mid-air,
and the wet ceramic thunk of the skull

on the curb of the poolside stone.
Then the deafening hush and the shouts,
the call for the ambulance,

the hotel workers shaking their heads
and speaking quietly in Spanish;
the medic kneeling to take the pulse—
the wild theatrical ride with the flashing lights.

Everyone knows that boys will kill themselves
as if it were just another kind of stunt
to plunge into the dark of the coma
and swim around down there, holding their breath

while up on the surface everyone waits,
while in the distance the phones of the families begin to ring,
the waiting room fills up with weeping girls,
the nurse steps out of surgery, unsnapping her latex gloves;

the newspaper editorial already hitting the streets
calling it a tragedy, a symptom, a waste,
spinning it this way or that,

though we're not really sure what it is about—
we only know that we somehow love the story
enough to repeat it,

and also that the story is a kind of sponge
that soaks everything up,

taking care of the mess—
the way the custodian moves his mop back and forth
on the patio of the Beachcomber Inn

as the boy and the girls and the palm trees by the road,
even the smell of suntan lotion and the
wild red light of the ambulance,

all disappear—

to be squeezed out again in another year—
splashed pinkly, spattering richly onto the ground,
fresh and familiar, because it is spring again.

ODE TO THE WEST WIND

Soon enough
it's going to be another kind of adventure entirely
for us to be dying all out of order,
waiting to see who's next, who a-
bruptly by surprise, and who's

psychically equipped to take
the nasty needles and the drips,
the Ellis Island of the waiting room,
the midnight disbelief.

Well, fortunately, we learned to like adventure
when we were wild and young,
when we cultivated a healthy
sense of unreality
that will be useful soon.
("Nurse, could you bring more
                mescaline to room 310?")

No, now is not the time
                for a faltering sense of style,
not now when you can hear your teeth
chatter like a Geiger counter
and see the lesions burning through your Technicolor skin,

now as the time machine accelerates
and you lean back and buckle up
with that famous dash of savoir faire
that made you perfect for your part

in this whimsical yet ballsy independent film
in which we play the wind.

HOW THE OLD POETRY HAPPENED

The sound of trees creaking in the dark above the house
                                    in the stillness before dawn,
like a ship's mast in a harbor where a hundred ships' masts sway
like a forest full of pines.

~

I had no beard when I started this journey.
Now I am hairy all over and my hair is gray and white
like a swirl of snowflakes and smoke.

~

In the dream, stranded on a cliff-face, I saw the ladder
swinging barely out of reach—dangled from the helicopter,
close enough to grab, but I was too afraid to jump for it,

even to save myself. When I woke, I said,
"Yes, that is true of me."

~

My father said he hated literary stuff
because it never says directly what it means.

But what about and how to say
these thousand mysteries that we live among?

~

Such a light dusting of snow, just enough that tires
leave clear tracks on the road.

~

Once, a white bird landed on a sailboat's mast
and was carried out to sea.

Let me be perfectly clear.
The boat was Time.
The bird was Me.

I DON'T ASK WHAT YOU'RE THINKING

You carry buckets of water to the plum tree in the yard
and pull weeds for an hour—then sit down at the kitchen table
and fill out long complicated insurance forms; or on the phone,
argue with a Blue Cross representative named Brian
about a charge on the bill from last October.

When I watch you sweeping the back porch,
I can see that you are already looking
for the next thing to do.

It may be there are times when we cannot afford an inner life.

It may be there are times when it would be a big mistake
to "get in touch" with your feelings

because they're big and dark and fatal, those feelings
like seaweed wrapped around the propeller of a ship
or a giant squid with great rubbery suction cups on its eighteen arms
waiting for the chance to pull you down.

Even when I catch you in the late afternoon
staring at the sky, I don't ask what you're thinking.
I don't want to interfere with the magnificent
discipline of your disconnection.

I feel like I am crouched down on my knees
looking through the round glass window in the door of the washing
    machine;
the dirty clothes churning around in there
furious and heavy, stained dark with the terribleness of life.
That's what I imagine of your feelings.

The last thing we need
is to go in there and get close to them.
Those feelings are not really our friends—when

what we are trying to do is to go on living,
to have the strength to keep the outer world in order,
and to keep holding onto it;

to stand at the counter with a knife in your hand,
cutting the vegetables.

CAUSES OF DEATH

In the records we can find
not one fatality
from reading the novels of Charles Dickens;

no obituary that reports
the cause of death
as "too much intuition."

So far no one mentioned in the *New York Times*
has perished from
grammatical errors.

No one—though it seems strange—
dead from "outrage and pity
at the mistreatment of nature."

So many gone down
from color of skin,
from lack of fair chances,
from lifelong deficiency of love.
If we are to be frank, let us say so.

Let us acknowledge that the popular singer
perished not from Jim Beam and cocaine
but a toxic infection
                    of fame and money.

Make it publicly known that Mr. Johansson
died after eighty-five years
of refusing all treatment
for his progressive condition of hate.

And then there is my sister,
that good-hearted woman,
who I like to tell people

relocated to Canada.
No reason to mention death.
If we don't hear from her much,

it must be because
she is very busy.
Somewhere in Ontario, possibly.

Outside of Banff, I believe.
I believe, and I remember,
and I miss her.

VIRGINIA WOOLF

On mornings like this I often think of her
lying in bed all day in her pajamas,
the room striped in sunlight and cats
like a painting by Matisse.

Virginia writing newsy letters to her friends:
"The light through fog is convalescent," she said,
and, "The main requirement for public life
is overacting."

On a morning like this,
when I walk the fields behind the house,
I feel that she is still alive,
sipping from her second pot of tea,
notebook propped up on her knees—

nose deep in language
like a thoroughbred horse,
like an endangered species
brought back from extinction.

I think of her and
I would like to know she is all right,
though I know she suffered terribly
from too much sight.

But who will talk to the petunias now
on Finchley Lane? Who will stand
and look out of the window for hours?
Who will tell the sunlight
                    not to be so vain?

Who will inform the piece of toast
on the small blue plate
with one bite taken out of it

that she will not be coming back?

FOUR BEGINNINGS FOR AN APOCALYPTIC NOVEL OF MANNERS

1.
Gabriel knew the end of the world would hurt business
and might very well mean his personal death,
but he also wondered how the company might
take advantage of the circumstances.
His dad had taught him well. Invest in oxygen?
Funeral parlors? Inflatable rafts?

2.
"I'm sorry to say this," said the computerized voice,
"but we need you to kill yourself, now." I was standing
in a public elevator by myself, so I was understandably startled.
Yet it was a woman's voice, so warm and considerate, so motherly,
that I quickly understood that this was the voice of the earth,
and also comprehended that her request was entirely reasonable,
from every point of view except mine.

3.
You looked so great in your end-of-the-world housedress and boots,
with your zinc sunscreen and radiation vest;
I was in love with you all over again.
After the fire and wrath, in spite of the destruction
and the widespread sense of shame and betrayal,
you still turned me on. I was attracted, as if you were the bomb
shelter and I was the bomb.

4.
Because of the virus, shaking hands and kissing
were forbidden in public, punishable offenses.
We had to decide
if we were for fraternity and love
or loyal to the government.
Doesn't that sound familiar?

In circumstances like this, I've learned to close my eyes and listen
for my deepest, innermost voice; it begins with a hum and rises,
the voice that says that the outer world,
even on a blue and sunny day, the unreal outer world
is already on its way, like a comet from outer space,

to completely destroy the inner.

THE POWER OF TRAFFIC

If you want to live in the city,
you have to understand the beauty of heavy traffic.
You have to love the *thunketa thunketa* of trucks at 4 a.m.
bringing meat and flowers into the markets and stores.

You have to witness the cement mixer
at the intersection of Willoughby and Grant
locked in a confrontation with the garbage truck,

neither guy willing to back down, both of them together
making one compound of a man
who keeps telling himself to shut up.

If you want to live in the city,
you have to see the feeder roads and interstates
from high above, at night, rhinestoned and seething,
spread out like the arms of an enormous squid

or like an alien intelligence, gathering facts,
or like the branching nervous system of a dinosaur,
all tangled up like a mixed metaphor.

You have to understand that traffic has taken the place in our lives
of the wind and the moon;
you have to hear the hum of the parkway as surf,
and the honking of horns in the morning
as a great migration of geese.

You have to lie in your bed at night with the window open
and listen to the music of the traffic;
the lonely howl of the ambulance siren
rushing toward the worst day in somebody's life,

and then for a moment the silence that follows
like the blank space hung between one heartbeat and the next,
as the cables swing gently in the wind,
and the light changes from green to red to green.

WEATHER OF PAIN

This week I'm reminding myself
to elevate my chin and walk with my head held straight,
attempting to follow the advice of the doctor,
who says I have spent too much time

with my face bent over papers and charts
so my C7 vertebra has become a protuberant knob
that sits in the upper back like a radio station
broadcasting on a channel called pain.

They say, "Listen to your body,"
but I have found that pain doesn't
speak in complete sentences;
its grasp of grammar is weak. Its pronunciation is unclear.

Pain is a sort of information
that arrives like a wave
and stays as a tidal action
surging around your foundation

in an erosive corrosive process
that slowly dissolves your notion
that you are more real than the world.
And pain has its mysteries, I think.

If you can hold out long enough
I suppose pain might eventually teach you
not to complain,
and if you are not killed by the tutorial,

you might come to see pain
                    as a kind of weather—
like the sun, the wind, and the rain

that fall through everything
and constantly change.

I can imagine a morning some day in the future
when I might wake up
and remove the blue knit hat I sleep in
and then the rest of my clothing

and go outside and stand in the pain
that is falling upward
from somewhere down inside of me.

I will stand there naked
as it flutters and fluctuates in waves
and paints all its colors on my skin
and how it dazzles and shines.

AUTUMN

From this town the summer people all go home.
The neighborhood houses are empty and echo-full.

In the crowns of the pines the crows rejoice
and the hedges start to show
                    their inner shapelessness.

It's cold, it's richly lonely,
it invites you into certain kinds of sin.

November is a giant hypodermic
from which hangs one glistening drop of nostalgia.

I sit by the window, and listen to newscasters
who are paid to de-emphasize their individuality

as the wind barely touches the trees,
tilting them forth then back.

In this kind of stillness, you should be able to find out
exactly what you feel,
                    if you feel anything.

You even might be able to see the space
                         between you and yourself

like a boat and the dock to which it is tied,
drawing, in a kind of deliberative drift, apart

and back together.

ON WHY I MUST DECLINE TO RECEIVE THE PRAYERS YOU SAY YOU ARE CONSTANTLY SENDING

Because first of all, I have a feeling that they didn't cost you anything,
and so I have to wonder: What is their actual market value?

For you, is the prayer like a radar-guided projectile
mounted on the hinged-together wings of several good intentions,
propelled by the flawed translation of a Rumi poem?

Anyway, my mailbox is already pretty much occupied for the season.
At the beginning of May, a big mother wren started moving in,
one mouthful of straw and twig at a time.

For three days, she flew in and out, in and out and in,
building a nest the size of a small soup bowl.
Then she sat on her eggs for two weeks, cooing and fluffing to keep
     them warm.
Then she was busy feeding her young.

I think the heat passing through that mother's body into her brood
has already surpassed the endoplasmic vibrational voltage
you've mentioned as a feature of the prayers you are sending me.

I understand that you are doing your best
to hoist yourself up toward a spiritual life,
even if it is through the doorway of a kind of pretending.

But if you really care, as you claim, please
will you kindly sit down and work your shit out?
Stop stealing reality from the world
and replacing it with make-believe!

The newspaper says that poorly aimed prayers
are causing flat tires on I-25.

The sandalwood incense blowing across the valley
is already causing cab drivers a lot of allergies.

So sit still and just look at the colors of the changing sky.
And could you stop burning so many candles, please?

My god, think how many hours and hours and hours—
think of how hard those bees worked
to make all that wax!

MISTAKEN IDENTITY LIBRARIAN SYNDROME

I think the pink-haired librarian has me mixed up with someone else.
Because she used to be so nice when she checked me out,
but now she is hard as a barcode machine
and chilly as the jar of iced tea in the employee fridge.

I think some other white-haired guy about my height must have
been caught last week putting art books under his shirt
or maybe defacing the biography of Sonic Youth.
Then my librarian got her face recognition in gear
and swapped our identities under the desk.

Well, not much you can really do about so many things.
No action you can take to fix or ferret this out
—when the question to a librarian, "What happened to our relationship?"
immediately triggers the Crazy Stranger Alert.

But I miss the friendliness of librarian Maureen
with the lavender forelock some would call pink
and the broad-striped Danish sailor shirts she favors.
And I pick my books more carefully now

knowing the wrong one could make things worse,
like *The Zurich Assassin* or *Dead by Dawn*.
But why do I feel bad when I've done nothing wrong?

As I stand before her and she scowls at the overdue screen
and does not look up when she stamps me out
—a victim of unpredictable patterns

in human weather
where the best option is to take your literature away
like a tuna fish sandwich in a brown paper sack

and have a nice day in spite of yourself,
with the hunch that you are involved
in a whole bunch of mistaken identities

you should be used to by now,
though knowing that so much of life
is just imaginary

doesn't make it easier
to lose something I had
and that I liked quite a lot,

and in fact had already counted
on renewing forever
without knowing it.

LANDSCAPE WITHOUT JASON

Now it is summer.

In the high school parking lot, the yellow bus
is waiting for the ones who failed in math.

Lilacs exude the perfume of a thousand former girlfriends,

and matter still surges like a tide,
bringing new things to the top—breath mints and broken promises,
short haircuts and greedy CEOs.

I am looking for some twine to bind up a tomato plant
so genetically enhanced
                                its big red bosoms are just about to break

its little stalk.

Now people have stopped crying
and it's like remembering you is voluntary.

Just outside, the pine pollen of year 2010
                                is marrying fresh varnish on the porch.

My head is next to the sink, in the everything drawer.
I don't have much to say.

I'm like the kid in the story, who had a crevice in the garden wall,
which got sealed over.

I've lost one of the places I tell things to.

WALK

Every day at about the same time, you take the same walk
with the sun coming up.
Through a gap in the fence you disappear.
I've seen how your boot-prints go up the slope

where they have worn a path by repetition.
And I assume each day that what you see is different.
The frost like dust on the juniper trees.
A toppled pine with its roots yanked up.

The coyote that runs, then stops on the ridge to look back.
Most of all, I suppose, it's the distance and the light
that you appreciate—the mountains changing
their appearance minute by minute,

from melon-rose to copper to grayish-green to blue.
I know the walks are part of your secret life.
I know there are a hundred things that you will never tell,
things that are not meant to be put into words.

Your walk is like a coin pushed into a slot.
I see you every morning slip through,
then drop like a wish into a well,
the wish being yourself, and the being alive that you've got.

SUCCESS

After a year of rehab and therapy, the country western singer
went back to writing songs; but he had changed.

Lyrics like "Good boundaries make a better kind of friend"
and "When you say goodbye, I feel so violated"

—they simply didn't have the punch of his best work.

~

In New York, Famous Joe's Pizza Parlor on Travis Street
is suing Joe's Famous Pizza on East Ninth Ave. for stealing its name.

The battle rapidly grows vicious. The courtroom smells
                                    of melted, burning cheese.
If he wins, Famous Joe says that his attorney will get free slices for life.

~

"Jesus had a great career," says one of the students on Monday morning,
reading out loud from his assignment;
then, sensing an uneasy silence—"Well, but he was famous, wasn't he?"

~

The mountain climber who actually made it to the summit,
the place so many of his friends had failed to reach,
got one great photograph, plus permanent damage
to nerves in his nose and his ears, both hands and feet.

~

Why don't you tell me about your life for a change?
Did you carry it carefully, like a brimful cup of water,
bound for a particular flower?

Or did you keep accidentally turning around
to look at something else,
and slosh it all over the place, like me?

DANTE'S BAR AND GRILL

In the middle of life, I found myself in a dark restaurant,
watching the round ass of the waitress
as I followed her across the thick red carpet
toward a table in the back,

obediently threading, with my party of four,
between the other tables with their
snow-white tablecloths and murmured conversations.

Around me were the hungry souls of those
dining on slow-roasted heritage potatoes
and organic free-range lamb garnished
with a sauce of rosemary and mint.

My guide murmured as she walked, "These are
ones who in life used immigrant babysitters,
disposable diapers,
and never read poetry;

whose single word in Italian was *mochaccino*—
you must not speak to them."
I dropped my face as she commanded

but understood I was among the sort
whose sins were no different from my own;
whose disproportionate good fortune I had shared;
whose faults I had subjected to merciless appraisal;
whose child-rearing histories I had recklessly critiqued.

It was night. Light trembled on their glasses
of dry white wine. I saw our long association
condemned me with these others
—not for my loyalty or love;

not that I would justify their ways;
they were simply the folk among whom
I had been dropped by fate at birth,

and being at heart a timid man,
I was going to stay with them
no matter what I was told,
even if it meant that we were going,
all of us, together, straight down to hell.

KING OF THE NIGHT

In the dark, I get up and
put on the clothes that come to hand.
Later I'll see what I'm wearing.

Outside, the neighborhood is exquisitely still,
enameled in moonlight,
enrolled in the School of Blue Silence.

As I pick up the paper,
I'm thinking about the phrase *finally realized*,
how inaccurate it is,

and also that I will probably
more or less from this point on
be confused exactly like this.

Then, from out of the shadows by the curb,
where he has been regally, invisibly
waiting all along,

quietly steps the cat,
and I say to him, as I always do, "You
are the King of the Night."

SIBERIA

In these final few months of my life,
I feel a little like a Russian poet
who's been exiled to a remote
village in Siberia;

all because of a remark I apparently made
at a party one night in Moscow,
where, to be honest, as I told the judge later,
vodka was the culprit, your honor.

What a journey this has turned out to be!
The old life impossibly far away,
nothing to read but the sky,
zero good-looking women on this train;
thrown like a rock into a time zone
before the existence of the telephone.

Now here I am in this shabby
                            outpost of empire;
twelve houses, three hovels, two barns;
four goats, a tubercular,
seems-to-be-starving cow, and
innumerable chickens.

It would be nice to think a kind of purification
was going on. Nice to make a joke
and say that these bumpkins
are probably paid by the government
to impersonate themselves;

but here each day is the same:
every dawn the blacksmith
striking his anvil like a hangover—
frightening the children awake,
scaring the birds from the trees.

Still, I have borrowed a stubby green pencil
from the three-fingered postmaster, Ivan.
Each day for an hour at least I write.
The outhouse is where I do my best work.

And in that sense, I wish to report, it's
not so bad: for I feel I have been artfully set down
in the perfect place for a poet:
on the very X of the paradox.

At night in my bed in the dark,
I feel around for it
under the tattered layers of quilt—
sometimes I can almost make out its shape
with my feet—

that life-and-death stuff
of which everyone knows
but people don't like to speak.

Since this is where I find myself,
I have pushed my objections aside;
I have ceased making plans for an escape.

Slowly, even as the autumn turns,
even as the leaves blaze and start to fall,
even as I slip into another night of pain,

I can feel myself gradually turning into
an informant. By what
government I am employed
I can't yet tell;

but I am making these notations for myself;
and I am warning you, my friends,
I will be filing my report.

ECONOMICA

The waiter in the expensive restaurant
gets tipped nine dollars for pouring a glass of wine.
The waitress in the hash joint
gets a dollar twenty-five for delivering

three plates of scrambled eggs with hash browns,
toast, Canadian bacon, biscuits and gravy,
plus medium OJs for two and coffee for everyone.

This is the condition of which Marx spoke,
which has forged the deformed world,
to which you are obedient

—as the bill arrives
and the credit card is run
and the receipt sticks out its little tongue

and you feel that small frisson which comes
from being ever so much on top of it
—as in the foyer of the restaurant, André

wishes you a very good evening, sir, indeed,
and softly clicks the heels of his black shoes;
as in the diner, with no one watching,

the waitress scrubs at a stain on the tabletop
and laughs at something
nobody can hear but her.

THE DECLINE OF THE ROMAN EMPIRE

Flaucus Timonius has the first heated toilet seat in District Eleven.
Only other members of the Senate are invited to try it.

His wife Octavia wears heels so high
she needs a ladder to get into them.

Marcus Gaius, a counsel from Gaul,
predicts a downturn in palanquin sales.
People are hanging onto their old palanquins longer, he says.

Tycho gets his face wrapped in blue Egyptian clay,
which he claims opens his pores.

A scandal reveals that Messenio's popular speeches
are written by an educated slave
and his clever insults by another.

Disposable diapers, immigrant nannies, edible thongs.
With great blocks of stone, the walls of the city are raised another meter.

Down the block, Caius Augustus is bragging about the new mind-control
    gizmo
he brought back from Alexandria.
You plug it in and it hums.

You'll never believe what happens next.
You stop thinking other people are real.
He calls it television.

CUISINE

All during dinner at the Italian restaurant,
David keeps checking his phone
to see if he is going to get laid later tonight
by a woman he met online two days ago—

deeply absorbed, working his quick thumbs over the tiny keys,
he's lining things up: the address for the Uber;
the color of the girl's apartment front door;

and I am eating my spinach salad, waiting for him to look up,
and wondering, *How much of this shit
do I have to put up with?*

Outside the rush-hour traffic keeps going by,
with a sound like the surging of surf,
and each time the kitchen door flaps open,

I can hear the waiters and cooks shouting to each other,
trying to keep the orders for chicken Alfredo straight.
The world of appetite unceasingly rolls on.

I remember the year that most of my friends stopped writing letters,
I mean physical letters that went in an envelope,
that required licking a stamp and walking someplace to mail.

I remember bathroom B on the cancer ward,
the only place on the sixth floor
where you could go to be alone,
pressing my face to the cool blue tile
in the middle of the night.

I remember the silence in my head
when I understood I was being told

that what I had was incurable,
understanding perfectly well that it was no one's fault,

and hating people anyway—
everybody, even my friends,
for not saving me.

THE INTERFAITH CHAPEL IS IN THE
SOUTH TERMINAL

The intercom tells me where to go:
up the elevator and down the narrow corridor
into the sanctum of the interfaith chapel,

where the stained glass catches the nondenominational light
and spreads it around
in some interfaith way.

Hanging on the wall, yes, there is a wooden cross
but also an equilateral triangle of aluminum
and a parallelogram made of brass,

and now it is an undiscriminating kind of peace
that begins to spread
across the causeway of my heart:

peace over my runways;
peace creeping through my terminal; peace
up into my observation tower—

I have a growing urge to
get down on my undereducated knees
and make an intersupplication

to a nonspecific supreme being—
and to her or him or it I say

my mind is broken;
I'm tired of being a prosthesis
for perpetual motion.

I will surrender all my frequent-flier miles
if you will help me

to find my tears and drink them.
If you will help me to reach that place

where I am already
awaiting my arrival.

HOMEWORK

I had to redrill the holes in the base of the downstairs door
a little higher so the rubber apron of the sweep
would not jam but barely brush against the floor

to keep cold rivulets of air from leaking in.
There is a right way to do things and
I would have done it that way the first time,

but I was in a hurry and grabbed the wrong tool—
that's how I came to gouge my second knuckle
and drip blood onto the rug,

then furiously kick the antique molding loose.
Sometimes I think I'm not really qualified for this job,
the job of my life, I mean,

and yet I keep on doing it,
with more enthusiasm than skill,
as if jamming things together and twisting them hard

was an Eastern philosophy,
which claims not that life is beautiful
but that jagged edges and dried blood

are part of being here.
The damage proves that we are real.
About beauty, I am not prepared to say.

My field is wobbly table legs
and spreading ceiling water-stains.
The truth swings a little crookedly,

it has a faulty seal
and lets outside air leak in.
At some point, it may need fixing.

READING WHILE SICK
IN THE MIDDLE OF THE NIGHT

In the corny, escapist historical novel I've been reading
to help me sleep at night—of medieval Saxon warriors, set in 600 AD;
after it has rained for three days, it finally stops—

and the warriors, named Helfgar and Siegfried and Sklar
climb out of their crude wooden huts
and get ready to cross the flood-swollen river.

Historically, I don't know what language they speak;
whether they are early Germans or Vikings or Celts;
I don't know the names of their heroes or gods or ghosts.

But they wrap their swords and their axes in bundles of oiled cloth—
and raise them over their heads
as they wade through the muddy waters or swim or flounder across to
    the other side.

The remarkable thing is that what they are doing
is exactly what I am doing—each medieval night
I hold my mind up like a bundle

out of reach of the pain—as I walk through
the chest-high wash of these waves that push
and tug at my life.

I have learned that it is possible,
the night drenched in the knowledge of death
that rises and falters and falls for hours.

I can hold my mind over my head
and fear does not touch that part of me,
and in the morning we will be there,

on the other side of the night,
like the bank of a river,
though it seems impossible.

HARBOR

We would swim out in the afternoons
when the tide was very high

at that special place in France,
swim out so far that our lives

seemed like clothes left upon the shore behind,

and floating in that cold brine I would have the odd sensation
of being right on top of time, held up on the brimming lip

of it,
but also floating on memory

of the tide before, and the one before—
so that swimming in that harbor day after day

we no longer could tell what day it was—
and swimming out was like going back
to a place so out of reach we could not fathom what it meant,

only that we were being released
into some element that was cold and clear,

as if pleasure was a thing we could be suspended in
forever without the fear of losing it—

something that given to us once, no matter what,
never can be taken back.

INCOMPLETION

In the blues song, the singer begs the doctor for a diagnosis.
Doctor, doctor, he sings, *tell me please, what is this pain inside of me?*
But as soon as the doctor tells him, he starts demanding a cure.

This great dry cold of winter in the mountains, parched blond of the
    expansive fields,
and huge black crows flapping through the mesquite trees.

Remember sex, which used to be so all-important?
And then children, and then success, and what comes next?

The boat rubs and chafes against the dock, held in place by rope.
The words of flattery or blame linger in your head for days.

Your fear that no one would tell you the truth was justified.
However, your fear that no one cared was incorrect.

"If I hadn't dropped out of cooking school," says Gretchen, happily,
"I would never have mastered my
                Sunday morning waffles for screaming kids,
which I feel is my greatest legacy."

Maybe it would be best to stop trying to finish the story.
It may be you're not missing anything.

The sun comes up out of the shrouded fog on the horizon.
The finches and sparrows quarrel at the feeder,
                        and their chests are dusty gold and red.

What is the name of the bird that always flies away
when it notices me watching?

Why, as it escapes me, does it continue to bother me?

SUNDAY AT THE MALL

Sweetheart, if I suddenly flop over in the mall one afternoon
while taking my old-person-style exercise,
and my teeth are chattering like castanets,
and my skull is going *nok nonk nok* on the terra cotta tiles
                                        of the well-swept mall floor;

my tongue stuck out, my eyes rolled up into my head—
don't worry, baby, we knew this kind of excitement
might possibly occur
and that's not me in there anyway—

I'm already flying backward, high and fast
into the big arcades and spaces of my green life
where I made and gave away and traded sentences with people I loved
that made us all laugh and rise up in
unpredictable torrents of fuchsia eruption.

Dial 911, or crouch down by the body if you want
—but sweetheart, the main point I'm making here is:
don't worry don't worry don't worry:

those wild birds will never be returning
to any roost in this world.
They're loose, and gone, and free as oxygen.

Don't despair there, under the frosted glass skylight.
Don't mistake this spastic conclusion for real.

Because, sweetheart, this life
is a born escape artist,
a migrating fever,
a convict tattooed in invisible ink,
without mercy or nostalgia.

It came down to eat a lot of red licorice
and to adore you imperfectly
and to stare at the big silent moon
and love as hard as it could,

then to swoop out just before closing time
right under the arm of the security guard
who pulls down the big metal grate
and snaps shut the lock in its hasp

as if it, or he, could ever imagine
anything that could prevent anything.

AMONG THE INTELLECTUALS

They were a restless tribe.
They did not sit in sunlight, eating grapes together in the afternoon.

Cloud-watching among them was considered a disgusting waste of time.

They passed the days in an activity they called "thought-provoking,"
as if thought were an animal, and they used long sticks

to poke through the bars of its cage,
tormenting and arousing thinking into strange behaviors.

This was their religion.
That and the light shining through the stained-glass ancestors.

They preferred the name of the tree
to the taste of the apple.

I was young and I wanted to prove myself,

but the words I learned from them transmuted me.
By the time I noticed, the change had already occurred.

It is impossible to say if this was bad.

Inevitably, you find out you are lost, really lost;
blind, really blind;
stupid, really stupid;
dry, really dry;
hungry, really hungry;
and you go on from there.

But then you also find
you can't stop thinking, thinking, thinking;

tormenting, and talking to yourself.

IN THE BEAUTIFUL RAIN

Hearing that old phrase "a good death,"
which I still don't exactly understand, '
I've decided I've already
had so many, I don't need another.

Though before I go,
I wish to offer some revisions
to the existing vocabulary.

Let us decline the pretense
of the hyper-factual: the
myocardial infarction; the *arterial embolism*;
the *postoperative complication*.

Let us forgo the euphemistic:
the "passed away"
and "shuffled off this mortal coil,"
as worn out and passive as an old dildo.

Now, if poetry can help, it is time to say,
"She fell from her trapeze at 2 a.m.
in the midst of a triple backflip
in front of her favorite witnesses."

Let us say, "In broad daylight,
Ms. Abigail Miller
conducted her daring escape
before life, that crook,
had completely picked her pocket."

It is not too late for some hero
to appear and volunteer
in the name of setting an example:

Let us say, "He flew with abandon,
and a joyous expression on his face,
like a gust of wind
or a man in a necktie
from the last dinner party he would ever have to attend."

To say, "He was the egg
that elected to break
for the greater cause of the omelet;
the good piece of wood
that leapt into the fire."

"Though grudging at first,
he fell like the rain,
with his eyes wide open,
willing to change."

PEACEFUL TRANSITION

The wind comes down from the northwest, cold in September,
and flips over the neighbor's trash receptacles.

The Halifax newspaper says that mansions are falling into the sea.
Storms are rising in the dark Pacific.

Pollution has infiltrated the food chain down to the jellyfish level.
The book I am reading is called *The End of the Ascent of Man*.

It says the time of human dominion is done,
but I am hoping it will be a peaceful transition.

It is one thing to think of buffalo on Divisadero Street,
of the Golden Gate Bridge overgrown in a tangle of vines.

It is another to open the door of your own house to the waves.
I am hoping the humans will be calm in their diminishing.

That the forests grow back with patience, not rage;
I am hoping the flocks of geese increase
                                        their number only gradually.

Let it be like an amnesia that we don't even notice;
the hills forgetting the name of our kind. Then the sky.

Let the fish rearrange their green governments
as the rain spatters slant on their roof.

It is important that we expire.
It is a kind of work we have begun in order to complete.

Today out of the north the cold wind comes down,
and I go out to see

the neighbor's trash bins have toppled in the drive.
I see the unpicked grapes have turned
                         to small sweet raisins on their vine.

I see the wren has found a way to make its little nest
inside the cactus thorns.

AFTERWORD

Over the spring and summer before he died, Tony gathered a group of poems—recent and older—into what he imagined as a chapbook, titled *Turn Up the Ocean*, his final collection. We discussed its shifting contents, aware that I would be the one to finish the book. It wasn't until spring 2020, when I spent a lot of time at home as a consequence of the pandemic, that I felt ready to address his papers—stacks of typed poems, margins crowded with scribbles, and the thicket of drafts in his computer—and resume the process of adding, subtracting, and reordering. In the quiet of our house, with the world outside nearly as silent, surrounded by Tony's papers and books, I completed *Turn Up the Ocean* for him. Possibly a few of the newer poems that I chose to add he would have considered not yet polished enough for a book. But to my mind, the roughness of these poems lends them their luminous intensity. In my expeditions through his drafts, I also discovered poems he had overlooked or forgotten that fit well into the more expansive collection that is this book. Tony revised his manuscripts almost as much as he revised poems; he felt that any version might be good enough, but none exactly right. No doubt he would want to make changes to some of these poems and to this published version of *Turn Up the Ocean*.

Kathleen Lee
Santa Fe, New Mexico
July 2021

ACKNOWLEDGMENTS

The American Poetry Review: "Butter," "Incompletion"

Copper Nickel: "Economica"

Five Points: "Turn Up the Ocean"

Green Mountains Review: "American Story," "Autumn," "Landscape without Jason"

Harvard Review: "Four Beginnings for an Apocalyptic Novel of Manners"

Love's Executive Order: "Gorgon"

New Ohio Review: "Success," "Sunday at the Mall," "Why I Like the Hospital," "Homework," "Siberia"

The New Yorker: "Among the Intellectuals," "Peaceful Transition"

Ploughshares: "Bible All Out of Order," "'On a Scale of 1–10,' Said the Nurse, 'How Would You Rate Your Pain Today?'"

Poet Lore: "Squad Car Light," "The Power of Traffic"

The Sun: "Immersion," "Nature Is Strong," "Illness and Literature," "On Why I Must Decline to Receive the Prayers You Say You Are Constantly Sending," "In the Beautiful Rain"

"Sunday at the Mall" also appeared in *The Best American Poetry 2020*, Paisley Rekdal, guest editor, and David Lehman, series editor, published by Scribner.

Very heartfelt thanks to Peter Harris for his astute and generous help in assembling this book and for his inimitable presence in our lives.

TONY HOAGLAND (1953–2018) was the author of seven previous collections of poetry, including *Priest Turned Therapist Treats Fear of God*; *What Narcissism Means to Me*, a finalist for the National Book Critics Circle Award; and *Donkey Gospel*, winner of the James Laughlin Award of the Academy of American Poets. He was also the author of four books on poetry, including *The Art of Voice: Poetic Principles and Practice* (with Kay Cosgrove), *Twenty Poems That Could Save America and Other Essays*, and *Real Sofistikashun: Essays on Poetry and Craft*. With Martin Shaw, he published *Cinderbiter: Celtic Poems*, versions of Irish, Scottish, and Welsh lyrics and tales. He received the Jackson Poetry Prize from Poets & Writers, the Mark Twain Award from the Poetry Foundation, and the O. B. Hardison, Jr. Poetry Prize from the Folger Shakespeare Library. He taught at the University of Houston and elsewhere.